Is This a Monster?

by SCARLETT LOVELL
and
DIANE SNOWBALL

Photograph Credits Frans Lanting/Minden Pictures: front cover, pp. 9,10; Mantis W.F./ O.S.F./© Animals Animals: pp. 3, 4; W. Gregory Brown/© Animals Animals: p. 5; Mickey Gibson/© Animals Animals: p. 6; Michael Fogden/© Animals Animals: p. 7; Patti Murray/© Animals Animals: p. 8; Rod Williams/Bruce Coleman, Inc.: pp.11, 21; Michael Townsend/Tony Stone Images: p.12; Larry West/Bruce Coleman, Inc.: p.13; J & L Waldman/Bruce Coleman, Inc.: p.14; Steve Solum/Bruce Coleman, Inc.: p.15; Joe McDonald/Bruce Coleman, Inc.: p.16; E. R. Degginger/Bruce Coleman, Inc.: pp.17, 20; Kim Taylor/Bruce Coleman, Inc.: p.18; Wolfgang Bayer/Bruce Coleman, Inc.: p.19; Zigmund Leszczynski/© Animals Animals: p. 22.

Designed by Mina Greenstein

Printed in China
09 10 11   11 10

Library of Congress Cataloging-in-Publication Data
Lovell, Scarlett.
    Is this a monster? / by Scarlett Lovell and Diane Snowball.
        p.   cm.
    Summary: Introduces "monsters" by first showing a monster-like part of an animal, then revealing the entire animal. Includes information and interesting facts about the animals.
    ISBN 1-57255-018-X (pbk. : alk paper). — ISBN 1-57255-019-8 (big book : alk. paper)
    1. Animals—Juvenile literature. [1. Monsters. 2. Animals. 3. Questions and answers.] I. Snowball, Diane. II. Title.
QL49.L89 1995
591—dc20
                                      95-4740
                                        CIP
                                        AC

Is this a monster?

No. This is a spider.

Is this a monster?

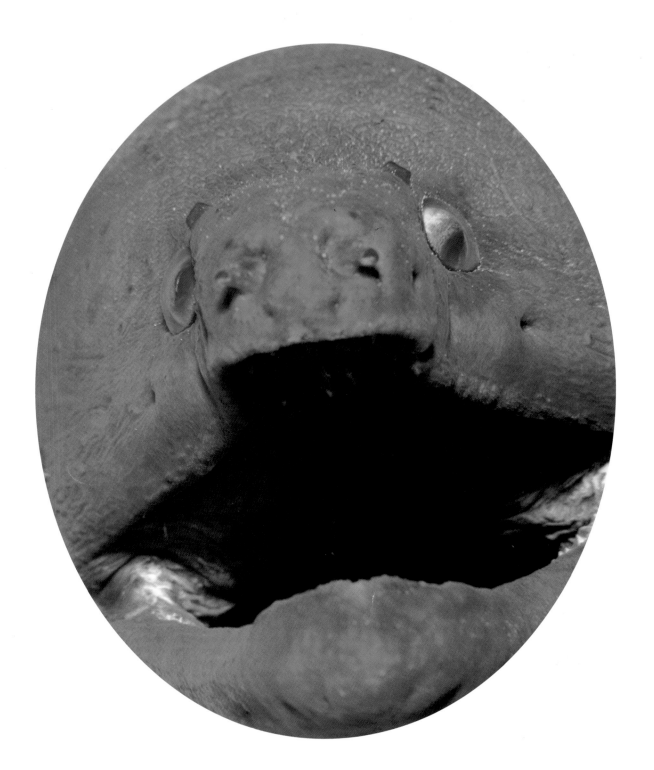

No. This is a moray eel.

Is this a monster?

No. This is a moth.

Is this a monster?

No. This is a gecko.

Is this a monster?

No. This is a mandrill.

Is this a monster?

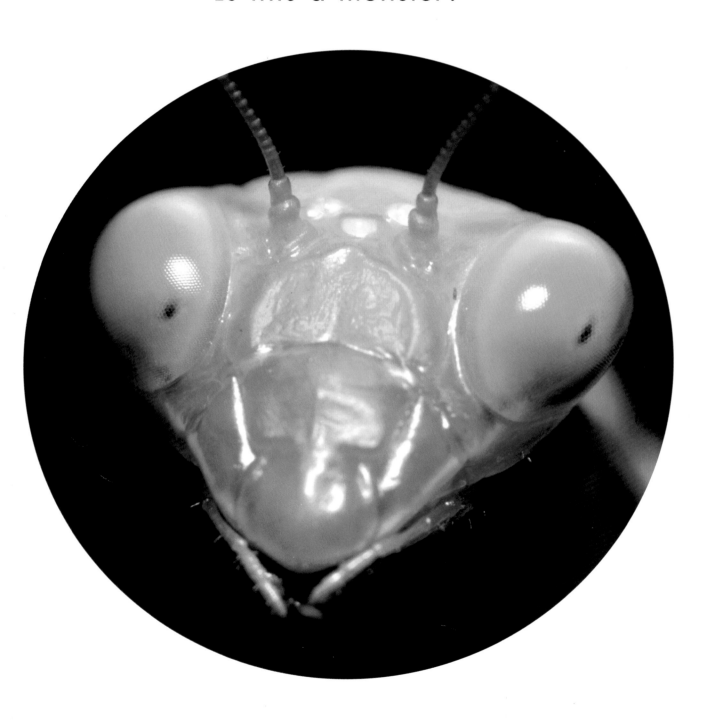

No. This is a praying mantis.

Is this a monster?

No. This is a turtle.

Is this a monster?

No. This is a bee.

Is this a monster?

No. This is a chameleon.

Is this a monster?

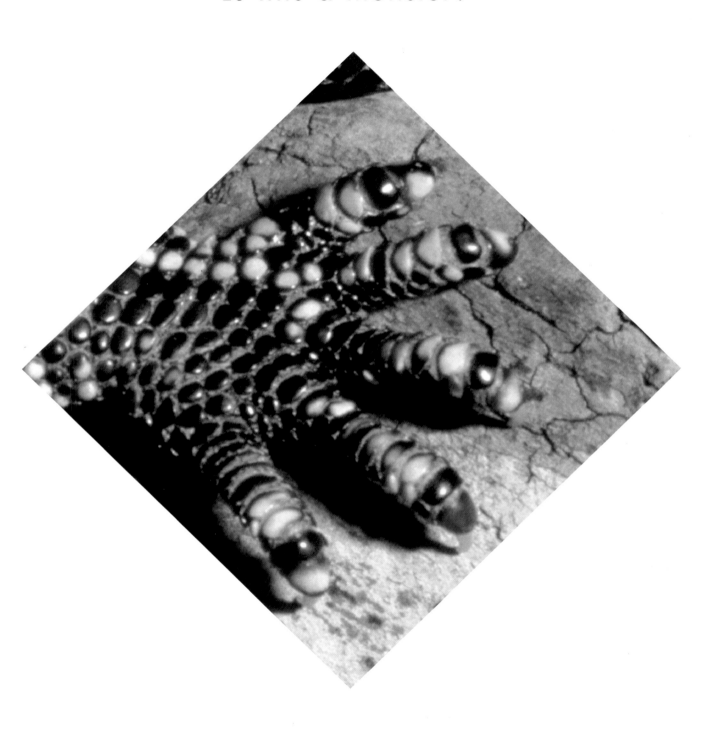

Yes! This is a gila monster.

ABOUT THE ANIMALS

NETCASTING SPIDER
Where found tropical areas
Size about 1 inch (2-½ cm) long
Interesting fact hangs upside down and throws its web over its prey

MORAY EEL
Where found around coral reefs in warm tropical seas
Size up to 6 feet (2 m) long
Interesting fact has long, sharp teeth but is not aggressive

HAWKMOTH
Where found throughout United States, southern Canada
Size from 1 to 2 inches (2 to 5 cm) long
Interesting fact moves its wings so fast when flying that it is just a blur

LEAF-TAILED GECKO
Where found Madagascar
Size about 8 inches (20 cm) long
Interesting fact has giant bulging eyes and excellent vision

MANDRILL (type of monkey)
Where found jungle of western Africa
Size about 3 feet (1 m) long
Interesting fact yawning is one way it shows it is upset

PRAYING MANTIS
Where found northeastern United States, southern Canada
Size about 2-1/4 inches (5-3/4 cm) long
Interesting fact when resting, folds it front legs as if in prayer

EASTERN BOX TURTLE
Where found on land throughout eastern North America
Size up to 7 inches (17 cm) long
Interesting fact can close both front and back openings
of its shell so it becomes enclosed within

BUMBLEBEE
Where found in temperate and northern areas
Size up to 1 inch (2-1/2 cm) long
Interesting fact thick hair protects it from the cold, but only
the queen survives the winter

CHAMELEON
Where found Africa, Madagascar, southern Europe,
southern Asia
Size from 1-1/2 inches to 2 feet (4 to 61 cm) long
Interesting fact changes skin color when the temperature
changes or if it is threatened

GILA MONSTER (type of lizard)
Where found desert of southwestern United States, northern
Mexico
Size about 2 feet (61 cm) long
Interesting fact one of only two lizards that are poisonous